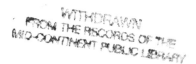

Josh Gibson

Nick Twemlow

the rosen publishing group's
rosen central

Published in 2002 by The Rosen Publishing Group, Inc.
29 East 21st Street, New York, NY 10010

First Edition

Library of Congress Cataloguing-in-Publication Data

Twemlow, Nick.
Josh Gibson / by Nick Twemlow.— 1st ed.
p. cm. — (Baseball Hall of Famers of the Negro leagues)
Includes bibliographical references (p.) and index.
Summary: Presents a biography of the powerful home run hitter and chronicles the history of African American participation in organized baseball, the formation of the Negro leagues, and racial politics in America.
ISBN 0-8239-3475-6 (lib. bdg.)
1. Gibson, Josh, 1911–1947—Juvenile literature. 2. Baseball players—United States—Biography—Juvenile literature. 3. African American baseball players—Biography—Juvenile literature.
[1. Gibson, Josh, 1911–1947. 2. Baseball players. 3. African Americans—Biography. 4. Negro leagues.] I. Title. II. Series.
GV865.G53 T94 2002
796.357'092—dc21

2001004143

Manufactured in the United States of America

Contents

Introduction   5

1. The Early Years   11

2. To the Smoky City   23

3. From Playground Legend to Pro   35

4. With the Grays   45

5. The Black Babe Ruth,
      the White Josh Gibson   61

6. The Early Death of a Star   77

7. Negro League Baseball Arrives   91

   Timeline   98

   Glossary   102

   For More Information   105

   For Further Reading   108

   Index   110

In a sixteen-year career that lacked the showmanship characteristic of the Negro leagues, Josh Gibson developed a reputation as a larger-than-life hitter that, according to many baseball historians, rivaled that of famed Yankee slugger Babe Ruth.

Introduction

osh Gibson is buried in Allegheny Cemetery in Pittsburgh, Pennsylvania. The flat tombstone marking his grave reads, simply, "Josh Gibson, 1911–1947, Legendary Baseball Player." Separating the years of his birth and death, in place of a dash, is a crucifix. Marking the site of the grave is a metal pole, maybe three feet tall, with a sign bearing Gibson's name attached to it.

George Herman "Babe" Ruth is buried in the Gates of Heaven Cemetery in Hawthorne, New York. One of baseball's most famous players lies in state, like a president. Two tall evergreen trees stand guard in front of a mausoleum. A giant stone sculpture of a saint with his hand on a little boy's head is flanked by two smaller stones, one engraved with the names of Ruth and his wife, along with their birth and death dates. The other bears a quote from the former archbishop of New York, Cardinal Spellman, which reads: "May the divine spirit that animated Babe Ruth to win the crucial game of life inspire the youth of America!" There is a giant baseball bat resting against one of the stones; several baseball caps and framed photos and various other tokens of fans' affections decorate the monument to Ruth.

In death, as in life, attention devoted to Ruth far outweighs that afforded to Gibson. During his brilliant career, Josh Gibson barely registered a blip on the American baseball radar screen. The man often called the "Black Babe Ruth" slipped through his short life barely noticed by a baseball-crazy American public. Admired by his fellow players, and perhaps the most powerful home-run hitter ever to put a bat to a ball, Gibson hit an estimated 900 homers over his career. Surprisingly, he was never able to attract the kind of huge audiences that came to see his former teammate and frequent rival, the colorful Satchel Paige. Both the press and fans knew of Josh Gibson, and undoubtedly many people came to watch a game just to see him hit. But Gibson mostly kept to himself and was a somewhat mysterious figure within the world of African American baseball.

So perhaps it is fitting that Gibson's grave site is simple, even plain. Though he may have been the greatest hitter the Negro leagues ever saw, Gibson died quietly—penniless and unhappy. This is not to say that he had a bland personality, or no complexity to him; indeed, as we shall see in the pages to come, the life of Josh Gibson was far from simple.

Legend has it that Gibson died of heart failure, but many baseball writers have said it was a broken heart. These writers contend that not getting the chance to play in the major leagues, against white players, is what broke Gibson's heart. While it is likely that Gibson's unfulfilled desire to cross the color line and play against white ballplayers left him with a heavy heart, his ongoing struggles with alcohol and drug addiction are what finally killed him. And this example serves to point out the difficulties of talking about Negro league players.

For years, sports writers and historians have described Negro league players and their accomplishments in heroic terms. Understandably, these writers hoped to correct years of racial injustice and celebrate the achievements of African American baseball players. But while it may make a good story, saying that Gibson died of a broken heart glosses over the difficulties in his life. The politics of baseball, which in turn hinged on the racial politics of America, affected the lives of African American baseball players. Gibson and many other players faced countless barriers during their playing careers. This is why we must look at Gibson's life with as unsparing an eye as possible. In order to understand the circumstances that led to Gibson's death at age thirty-five in the early hours of January 20, 1947, we have to understand how African American participation in organized baseball began, even before the formation of the Negro leagues.

A view of Knickerbocker Village, where the Knickbocker Base Ball
Club originated, in New York City's Lower East Side in 1932

The Early Years

Baseball historian Harry Simmons notes that the first official all-African American baseball game took place in 1860 in Brooklyn, New York, fourteen years after the first recorded all-white baseball game took place between the Knickerbocker Base Ball Club of New York and the New York Base Ball Club at Elysian Fields in Hoboken, New Jersey, on June 19, 1846. In 1960, the two African American teams, Weeksville of New York and the Colored Union Club, played a full nine-inning game, with Weeksville winning 11–0.

At this stage, baseball was more a form of upper-class leisure activity than a sport. White teams were stocked with wealthy gentlemen, and the African American teams were mostly filled with former Union army soldiers. Games were often an excuse for picnics and dances. Women, possibly attracted by the social features of the games, came to the games in great numbers.

The new game of baseball, which was similar to the British game of cricket, had rules barely recognizable by today's standards. Pitchers threw underhand, from a distance of forty-five feet (rather than today's sixty feet, six inches) from the batter. This placed the pitcher dangerously close to the hitter. And pitchers tried to get the batters, or "strikers" as they were called, out on four strikes. Fly balls caught were an out, but a foul ball caught on one bounce was also an out. Players played bare-handed, and games would be over if one team scored twenty-one runs.

By 1865, a loose organization of African American baseball teams sprung up across the East and throughout the Middle-Atlantic states. The teams were composed mainly of soldiers who had fought in the Civil War. Among the teams were the Monitor Club of Jamaica (New York), the

Bachelors of Albany (New York), the Excelsiors of Philadelphia, and the Unique Club of Chicago.

By the late 1860s, the Pythians, a team formed by two ex-cricket players and promoted by former army major Octavius V. Catto, formed in Philadelphia. The team quickly became known as a powerhouse, soundly beating most of the other African American baseball teams. Finding a ball field for African American games in Philadelphia could be difficult, so the Pythians often invited teams to play their games out of town.

The NABBL and the NAPBBL

The popularity of baseball—as played by whites—was booming. Founded in 1858 to protect the interests of amateur baseball in New York City, the National Association of Base Ball Players (NABBL) had grown into a national organization. Members would pay dues and the NABBL would set rules and admit teams into the association. Although the association's rules were haphazardly adopted, the NABBL provided baseball with a national public image. One issue not discussed was integration—the question of whether teams with African American players would be allowed to join, and thus play in, the association. Doubtless the question wasn't an issue because the answer was already clear, as American society at large was segregated.

The brash promoter Octavius Catto decided to broach the question of integration in 1867. He dispatched Raymond C. Burr as his representative to the NABBL's annual convention in Philadelphia to ask for official recognition of the Pythians team. Though the white Philadelphia Athletics seconded Catto's petition, the court of white baseball ruled Burr out of order. The association issued the following statement: "It is not presumed by your Committee that any club who have applied are composed of persons of color, or any portion of them; and the recommendations of your Committee in this report are based upon this view, and they unanimously report against the admission of any club which may be composed of one or more colored persons." The association made this move, it claimed, not as a sign of racial prejudice but to avoid "subjects having a political bearing."

African American baseball experienced moderate successes over the next couple of years, including several white-versus-African American games that were wildly popular and financially successful. Unfortunately, the death of Octavius Catto, who had become a powerful African American rights activist in Philadelphia, signaled the end of organized African American baseball. Catto, who was murdered at the age of thirty-one by a white man, had been African American baseball's biggest promoter. Even the Pythians folded, and African American baseball quietly faded away.

Oddly enough, over the next twenty years, white baseball offered the only (albeit limited) opportunities for African American ballplayers. The creation of a professional organization, the National Association of

Moses Fleetwood Walker played major league baseball in the late nineteenth century before African Americans were banned from the game.

Professional Base Ball Players (NAPBBL), weakened the power of the NABBL. The NAPBBL was intent on changing the amateur atmosphere of baseball. They hoped to turn it into a profitable, organized business.

African American teams were nonexistent in the association, but a few African American players managed to find their way onto teams. In 1884, Moses Fleetwood "Fleet" Walker, a college-educated ballplayer, became the first African American to play in the majors. John "Bud" Fowler became baseball's first widely known African American player when, at the age of fourteen, he played second base for a white team in New Castle, Pennsylvania.

Fowler, a highly accomplished player, carried the extra burden of having to constantly prove himself to his white counterparts, a recurring theme for African American players for years to come. An African American player of this era faced racism in the form of white major league players, managers, owners, and fans. A silent "gentleman's agreement" between major league clubs made the prospect of an African American player playing professional baseball exceptionally unlikely. Many white executives simply agreed to this policy without putting it in writing. Some team owners, motivated more often by their desire to win than any sense of justice, kept African American players on their teams, but put themselves at great risk by doing so.

But the few African American men playing in the minor and major leagues, such as Fowler and Walker, could not be ignored. Quite simply, they played some of the best ball anybody had ever seen in the game's then brief history. Fowler's considerable skills forced even white newspaper reporters to notice him. In 1885, *Sporting Life* magazine called him "one of the best general players in the country . . . If he had a white face, he would be playing with the best of them."

Some African American business leaders, impressed by the glowing praise players such as Fowler and Walker received in several white newspapers, attempted to put together leagues of African American teams. Among the limited successes in these attempts was the Southern League, composed of ten teams from across the South. The league was formed in 1886 and played out one full season before folding the next year. Financially unable to continue, the league did revive interest in all-African American professional teams. Over the next few years, the biggest presence of African American ballplayers came in the form of an independent team, the Cuban Giants.

African American players who played multiple seasons of organized baseball in the nineteenth century

- John Fowler (8)
- Moses Walker (7)
- George Stovey (6)
- Frank Grant (6)
- Sol White (5)
- Jack Frye (5)
- Richard Johnson (4)

The Cuban Giants

Formed in 1885, the Giants were a team of African American players who had formerly worked as waiters and porters at the Argyle

Hotel in Long Island, New York—not in Cuba.
By calling the team "Cuban," the team's white
financial backers hoped to improve the team's
chances of appealing to white audiences. While
most whites dismissed the thought of watching
an African American team play, promoters
hoped that some white fans might come to see
black baseball players from Cuba. As these
players were supposedly foreign-born, white fan
support did not entail breaking the rules of
segregation. The players tried to act like they
were from Cuba. This acting often took the form
of babbling incoherent "Spanish sounding"
words on the playing field.

Initially created to entertain white vacationers,
the team, under the guidance of white promoter
John F. Lang, turned professional and went on to
play as barnstormers. Barnstormers were teams
who traveled across the country, from small towns
to big cities, playing against any willing opponent.
These teams often played many games in one day,
and just as often played against the biggest and
best white teams of the time. In the absence of a

proven league, barnstorming became the only way for African American baseball teams to play regularly and earn money.

At the same time, players like Fowler and Walker were playing in the International League, composed mostly of teams from New York. African American players were often subject to hostility from fans, opposing teams, and even their own teammates. Many white-only teams would withdraw from a game against a team that fielded even one African American player.

If they did play, many players on whites-only teams attempted to injure African American players. The practice of a base runner sliding forcefully into second base and aiming his spiked shoes at the second baseman developed during this time. White players hoped to injure African American player Horace Phillips. Phillips would later strap wooden splints around his shins for protection.

The early history of African American baseball is part mystery, part myth, and wholly bound up in the question of race in America. The end of the Civil War did not mean the end of racism and inequality in America, nor did the signing of the Compromise of 1887 by the United States Congress and President Grover Cleveland. Instead, these acts officially ended Reconstruction and removed all legal obstacles to Jim Crow laws in the South. The effect was to reinforce racial segregation, particularly in the South. As the leading newspaper of the North, the *New York Times,* wrote, "Northern men no longer denounce the suppression of the Negro vote [in the South] as it used to be denounced in the Reconstruction days. The necessity of it under the supreme law of self-preservation is candidly recognized." Finally, the 1896 Supreme Court decision in *Plessy v. Ferguson* supported "separate but equal" public accommodations. Due to prejudice and discrimination, though, such accommodations were separate but wholly unequal.

To the Smoky City

In 1996, Josh Gibson, along with Satchel Paige and James "Cool Papa" Bell, were featured on the cover of a Wheaties box. This honor has become a rite of passage for many athletes, and in this case was in recognition of the seventy-fifth commemorative year of the Negro leagues. Given the long distances Josh Gibson traveled in his life—from sandlot legend to Negro league great, around the diamond and across the country—and the obstacles he faced, such as racism and poverty, Gibson would have good reason to smile at this unofficial "crowning."

Life in the South

By 1900, life for African Americans in the South was one of low wages, sixty- or seventy-hour

Josh Gibson, catcher for the Homestead Grays, crouches as he holds the baseball in his mitt during a game at Forbes Field in Pittsburgh, Pennsylvania, in August 1942.

workweeks, and little more than hope. Though the end of the Civil War and the subsequent era of Reconstruction had freed African Americans from their slaveholders in the South, the roots of racism ran deep throughout all of America. Jim Crow laws became a way to keep whites and African Americans separated.

From the 1880s well into the 1960s, a majority of American states enforced segregation through such laws. Across the country, these laws marginalized African Americans. In Alabama, for example, African Americans could not lawfully dine in the same room in a restaurant as whites, nor could they use the same restroom facilities. Interracial marriages were declared illegal in Arizona. If an African American family wanted to attend the circus in Louisiana, they would purchase their tickets at a different booth than white people, and would watch the show in an entirely different tent.

Though the effect of Jim Crow laws was felt most deeply in the South, northern states often passed Jim Crow laws, too. In fact, the state of

Massachusetts enacted the first such law in 1841, forbidding African Americans and whites to travel in the same railroad car. But many African Americans still considered the North a better place to live because the growing industrial centers found in such places as Pittsburgh, Pennsylvania, and New York City, offered many opportunities for work.

Up North

It was this promise of work that led Josh's father, Mark Gibson, to uproot his family from their home in Buena Vista, Georgia, a village close to Atlanta, and take them to Pittsburgh. A sharecropper, Mark Gibson had heard the stories of prosperous African American communities forming in these cities. In 1921, he set out alone for Pittsburgh, then known as the Smoky City, and tried to gain employment in the massive steel industry there.

Shortly after arriving, he found a job with the giant Carnegie-Illinois Steel plant. Three years later, he sent for his wife, Nancy, and three children, Josh, (born December 11, 1911); Jerry, (born in 1914); and a daughter, Annie, (born in 1917). The family moved into the Pleasant Valley neighborhood on the city's North Side. Their split from the South was complete.

For Josh Gibson, Pittsburgh offered a vast playground of streets and sandlots, and he soon established himself as one of the neighborhood's best athletes. He was stocky and thick, but a fast runner and powerful swimmer. And though he had played baseball a few times in Georgia, there were numerous opportunities for him to pick up a bat and swing at baseball games in Pleasant Valley.

The lure of baseball, and his growing skill at the game, would soon lead Josh out of school. As he said much later in his life, "The greatest gift Dad gave me was to get me out of the South." And since Josh was nearing his full size of six feet one inch and 215 pounds, he was already a presence on the field. Having completed the fifth grade in Georgia, Josh continued school in Pittsburgh in the Allegheny Pre-Vocational

School, where teachers steered him toward electrical studies. But as the professional prospects for African American baseball players increased, along with the possibility that a young African American boy could become a professional ballplayer, the lure of the game became irresistible. For Josh and other young boys in Pleasant Valley, the team that filled their dreams was known as the Homestead Grays.

The Grays

Located just east of Pittsburgh, Homestead, Pennsylvania, is a steel mill town. In the early part of the twentieth century, many steelworkers were also great ballplayers. The best of them played for the Murdock Grays—an integrated team that challenged, and usually beat, other local teams. But the team was transformed that year when a young man fresh out of Penn State University named Cumberland Willis Posey ("Cum" to his teammates), joined them. He was made captain within two years. Posey also worked at organizing the Grays, by then called the Homestead Grays, into a semiprofessional team.

Posey was a creative and fierce manager and promoter. He successfully fought to repeal the ban on playing Sunday ballgames. In this way, he increased the amount of money he and his team could earn. This increase in revenue enabled Posey to put his players on salary by 1922. When Posey signed the well-known African American pitcher Smokey Joe Williams, who brought with him a storied history from his play with African American teams in Chicago and New York, the Grays were headed for the big time. They became the most popular African American team in Pennsylvania.

Under Posey's firm guidance, by the late 1920s the Grays became a profitable organization. The importance of their success, on and off the field, cannot be underestimated. African American fans packed games to cheer their no-nonsense brand of baseball. Their winning ways made them heroes to the kids of Homestead and Pittsburgh, including Josh Gibson.

Cumberland "Cum" Posey was the driving force that made the
Homestead Grays into one of the most successful and enduring
teams of the Negro leagues.

The Negro National League

Interestingly, Posey and the Grays were not a part of organized African American baseball, which was headed at that time by Rube Foster, a Chicagoan who had once been a talented pitcher. Foster turned to organizing and owning teams in Chicago in the early part of the 1900s. Foster aimed to create a Negro league, composed of established African American teams from northern cities, that would equal the white baseball leagues.

The Negro National League (NNL) consisted of Foster's own Chicago American Giants, the Cuban Stars, the Dayton Marcos, the Chicago Giants, the Indianapolis ABCs, the Kansas City Monarchs, the Detroit Stars, and the St. Louis Giants. It is interesting to note that over two dozen African American baseball teams were called the Giants, both before this time and after. Why? Because many newspapers refused to run pictures of African American people, so when readers saw the word "Giants" they recognized it as a code word for a game involving an African American team.

The NNL experienced the usual growing pains a new business suffers, but it persisted and succeeded as no other African American baseball league had before. A rival organization, the Eastern Colored League (ECL), formed in 1923. Instead of joining forces with Foster's NNL, the ECL fought bitterly for the same players, franchises (teams), and fans. Over the next decade, this competition nearly destroyed both leagues.

What was Cum Posey doing with his Homestead Grays during all of this? He was sitting back, observing this competition and the destructive effects it was having not only on the leagues' survival but on all of African American baseball. He was keenly aware that if the Grays joined one or the other league, his own control of the team would weaken. In fact, Foster was losing control of his own league, as he suffered from mental illness. By 1926, he was unable to function from day to day. He was hospitalized, and died at the age of fifty-one in 1930.

Rube Foster was the founder of the National Negro League, which would become the greatest of all the Negro leagues.

Foster had given African American baseball a forceful and necessary push. Though the NNL folded in 1932, as did the Eastern Colored League four years earlier, a new league emerged: the American Negro League. Cum Posey finally decided that his Grays would join. This marked the beginning of Posey's impressive political influence on all Negro league baseball.

Although he is most often heralded for his prowess with the baseball bat, Josh Gibson was no slouch as a catcher.

From Playground Legend to Pro

osh Gibson left Allegheny Pre-Vocational School at the age of sixteen, having completed the ninth grade. He took up various jobs, apprenticing in an air brakes manufacturing plant, moving on to a steel mill, even working in a department store. Leaving school was probably not a difficult decision for Gibson, though he was a mild-mannered and likeable teenager by all accounts. But his family didn't place an emphasis on education, and a family such as his, intimately familiar with the poverty of the South, was more interested in making ends meet. Indeed, the Gibsons learned that African American poverty was not just a Southern problem, but an American one.

By 1927, Gibson had established his reputation as a ballplayer in the sandlots scattered about Pleasant Valley. In fact, Gibson's entry into organized baseball came that year, when he joined a North Side team called the Pleasant Valley Red Sox; shortly thereafter, he joined an all-African American recreational team. He played catcher, the position he would play for the rest of his baseball career. Because of his considerable size and strength, as well as his quickness and keen reflexes, Gibson was well suited for the position. The following year, Gibson helped organize the Crawford Colored Giants along with Harry Beale, another North Side player. Gibson also played for the team.

The Craws

The Crawfords played a tougher, more skilled game of baseball than most sandlot teams. While many of Pittsburgh's finest young players were on the team, the Homestead Grays remained a cut above. The Craws, as they were sometimes called, did attract large crowds. Most of their games were played at Ammon Field on the North Side. Instead of purchasing tickets for admission, game organizers passed a hat around to collect small donations from the fans. The money they collected was used to pay the players. On a good day, there might be a few extra dollars in their pockets.

The Crawfords played as many as a hundred games in a summer. They established a reputation in the African American baseball world, even getting a mention every now and then in the Pittsburgh's African American newspaper, the *Pittsburgh Courier*. Nevertheless, they made little money.

The Great Depression that began in 1929 had a severe impact on organized African American baseball. A team like the Craws suffered greatly, as fans had little money to donate. People still enjoyed watching games, but an African American team could no longer expect more than a penny or two, if that, from spectators.

But in 1930 Gibson was still playing ball, smashing home runs all over Pittsburgh as the full-time catcher for the Colored Giants. He hit home runs farther than anyone else playing at the nonprofessional level. Legend of his power spread throughout the state of Pennsylvania. His home runs were sometimes written about in the *Courier*, bringing Gibson to the attention of many people, including the ones behind the famed Homestead Grays. As Judy Johnson, manager of the Grays in 1930, said of Gibson: "I had never seen him play but we had heard so much about him. Every time you'd look in the paper you'd see where he hit a ball 400 feet, 500 feet. So the fans started wondering why the Homestead Grays didn't pick him up. But we had two catchers. Buck Ewing was the regular catcher, and Vic Harris, an outfielder, used to catch if we were playing a doubleheader."

A Student of the Game

Much of what made Gibson a great ballplayer, and what separated him from most of his teenage friends playing in the sandlot leagues, was his intense study of the game. Gibson buzzed like a fly around as many games as he could watch. He studied the technical aspects of the game: pitching angles, batters' stances, throwing movements, and so on. Less interested in watching towering home runs soar out of the ballpark, Gibson liked to watch the players to see how they positioned themselves. He noticed how they changed position as each new batter approached the plate. Baseball was, Gibson realized, a game of strategy.

Gibson observed catchers in particular. He watched how they shifted their feet, talked to the infielders, giving them instructions; he heard the banter catchers often took up with the batters in order to get inside their heads. His fascination with the game also extended to hitting. While he studied batters, his talents at the plate gave him confidence that he was close to having all of the tools he needed to be a great hitter.

Gibson's hitting style, in contrast to many African American players of his era, was nearly perfect. Many great African American players

New York Yankee Lou Gehrig, after whom Josh Gibson patterned his batting, watches the flight of a fly ball off his bat during the 1937 World Series.

had never had the opportunity to learn the fundamentals of hitting form from a hitting coach, and instead picked up their style from watching sandlot games and adopting the bad habits of other players. Gibson learned to hit in the same way he learned to catch: he studied, studied, studied.

Gibson patterned his style after that of the Yankees' first baseman, Lou Gehrig, whom Gibson felt was the most polished hitter of his day. Perhaps Gibson's only defect was his batting stance—an upright, flat-footed posture that he didn't really budge from when he swung the bat. But even this flaw was corrected not long into his professional career. His technical skill, combined with his unparalleled power and speed, made him a menace.

Gibson was not only a great home-run hitter, but a good overall hitter as well. He reached base often. Gibson had great courage at the plate, never letting a ball pitched at his head or an opposing catcher's remarks keep him from his task.

Homestead Grays' catcher Josh Gibson crouches near home plate
before the start of a Negro league game in 1931.

Perhaps the greatest part of Gibson's legend is the many myths and stories regarding the length of his home runs. One tall tale has it that he hit a ball out of sight one day only to have it reappear the next day. The umpire supposedly remarked, "Yer out! Yesterday, in Pittsburgh!" There are more believable stories of games being stopped midway to enable officials to measure one of Gibson's homers. The mayor of Monessen, Pennsylvania, did so one day, measuring one at a distance of 512 feet, a homer Gibson would later recall as the farthest he had ever hit. From New York's Yankee Stadium to Cincinnati's Crosley Field to Cleveland's Municipal Stadium, Gibson hit home runs farther than anyone.

Unlike many of today's baseball players, who celebrate as they round the bases after hitting a home run, Gibson played the game with a natural modesty. While his withdrawn nature dignified him among his peers, it would later hamper his contract negotiations.

Satchel Paige of the Kansas City Monarchs was one of a few pitchers against whom Josh Gibson did not have an impressive batting record.

With the Grays

Gibson wasn't impossible to put out, but his talents frustrated many opponents. Then again, certain pitchers did seem to "have his number"; that is, they were able to put him out more often than not. Among them were Teddy "Big Florida" Trent of the American Giants, and Chet Brewer of the Chicago American Giants and the Kansas City Monarchs. But even Brewer never really believed he had any success with Gibson, saying, "He could hit any pitch to any field. The only way to pitch to him was to throw the ball low and behind him."

And, of course, the legendary Satchel Paige, probably the only Negro league player more famous than Gibson, got the best of Gibson on a regular basis. Gibson said that his hits off Paige were "few and far between." A duel ensued when the two, who would later become teammates for a few seasons, faced off. Their famed showdowns fill African American baseball history and created some of the most dramatic moments in the game. For all of Gibson's respect for Paige's talent as a pitcher, Paige recognized Gibson's ability to turn things around in a hurry. "You look for his weakness and while you're lookin' for it he liable to hit forty-five home runs," Paige once said.

Gibson and the Grays

The myth and legend of Josh Gibson and his baseball skill began on the sandlots of Pleasant Valley. But the story, or stories, of how he became a member of his favorite team, the Homestead Grays, is the most complicated and enduring tale of all. According to legend, it was a series of freak accidents at a Grays night game that led Josh Gibson to the team.

Grays manager Judy Johnson tells one version of the story. Gibson started with the team in Pittsburgh on July 25, 1930, during a game between the Grays and 1929 Negro National League champions the Kansas City Monarchs. It was a night game under the unsteady lights of the Monarchs' new portable lighting system.

Johnson notes: "Joe Williams was pitching that night and we didn't know anything about lights. We'd never played under 'em before, and we couldn't use the regular catcher's signals, because if he put his hand down you couldn't see it. So we used the glove straight up for a fastball and the glove down—that was supposed to be the curve. Some was Joe Williams and the catcher [getting] crossed up. The catcher was expecting the curve and Joe threw the fastball and caught him right there, and split the finger. Well, my other catcher was Vic Harris and he was playing the outfield and wouldn't catch. So Josh was sitting in the grandstand, and I asked the Gray's owner, Cum Posey, to get him to finish the game. So Cum asked Josh would he catch, and Josh said, 'Yeah, oh yeah!' We had to hold the game up until he went into the clubhouse and got a uniform. And that's what started him out with the Homestead Grays."

As the story goes, Gibson didn't get a hit that night, but he made no errors behind the plate. This was quite a feat, given that Gibson was still a raw, unformed player, and eighteen years old to boot. Gibson stayed on with the team, progressing very quickly as a catcher and hitter.

A more likely version of how Gibson ended up playing for the Grays claims that Cum Posey knew of Gibson and told him to be prepared to play in a Grays game at any time. Gibson made his debut during a twilight doubleheader against Dormont, a white semiprofessional team. Some of the particulars mirror Johnson's account: Buck Ewing did split a finger, and Posey did turn to his backup, Vic Harris, to catch until Gibson could be reached and arrive at the field. Posey had Harris's brother taxi over to Ammon Center, where Gibson was in the middle of a game playing for the Crawford Giants. Gibson immediately withdrew from that game. After Gibson arrived, Posey put him into the Grays game with little fanfare. Whichever story is true, Gibson did join his beloved Grays that year. He split catching duties with Ewing and learned the art of "receiving," as catching is sometimes called, on the job.

A Homer a Day

The stint with the Grays began Gibson's professional baseball career. Gibson spent a great deal of time traveling with the team across the country, and his teammates became more familiar to him than the fading image of his father, mother, siblings, and old friends on the North Side of Pittsburgh. This separation, especially from his family, became a major theme in Gibson's life. Barnstorming was the only choice Gibson and all African American players had if they wanted to make a living playing the game.

Though Gibson eventually developed into one of the greatest hitters in the history of baseball, he was still in need of development when he joined the Grays. But thanks to his single-mindedness about all things baseball, and his terrific—if raw—skills, he quickly became a star. W. Rollo Wilson, a writer for the *Philadelphia Independent,* summarized neatly what many were saying about Gibson at this early stage in his professional career: "Well, the kid could catch and did catch and is still catching. He's green yet but the ripening process is moving apace. He has not mastered the technique in throwing to second base but he kills off all the fast boys who try to steal. His stance at the plate is worse than Pimp Young's [another Gray's catcher] but he gets his base hits. His motto is— 'a homer a day will boost my pay.'"

The papers labeled him "Samson" after the famed Biblical strongman. Gibson's huge appetite for food, especially vanilla ice cream and hot dogs, was well known. Although he gained more and more attention, he always remained focused on the game. During his first season with the Grays, Gibson hit a home run in Yankee Stadium in the season-ending series against a good team, the New York Lincoln Giants. The home run reportedly traveled 500 feet into the bullpen in left field—a drive fans would claim for years was one of the longest home runs ever hit there, even longer than any by Babe Ruth or Mickey Mantle. Some people contend that the shot traveled out of the stadium, a feat no one had ever accomplished.

Personal Woes

It was in 1931 that Gibson endured serious personal problems. He had met Helen Mason, who was from the Hill District in Pittsburgh. A few months younger than Josh, Helen became pregnant just after her seventeenth birthday. She and Josh married. Though still working an assortment of odd jobs, Gibson was quickly making baseball his main focus.

This series of photographs captures what many considered to be
Josh Gibson's near-perfect swing.

The two lived in relative comfort and peace with Helen's parents. That August, Helen went into a difficult labor at Pittsburgh's Magee Hospital, and after delivering twins, lapsed into a coma and died a few hours later.

The baby girl, Helen, and boy, Josh Jr., were a welcome addition after Helen's death, but the children were raised primarily by Helen's parents, as Gibson had little time to care for them. As Josh Jr. got older, he served as a bat boy for some Grays' home games. Though a source of conflict for Gibson over the course of his career, his inability to care for and see his children became a matter of fact. He was, for all intents and purposes, an absentee father until the day he died. Gibson's devotion in life was to baseball and little else, a fact that his family endured.

That fall, Gibson began what would become a yearly ritual of cross-country exhibition games against white major league "all-star" teams. These teams were usually composed of a haphazard collection of forgettable white players teamed with a top-name star or two, such as pitcher Dizzy Dean or hitter Jimmie Foxx.

The games served to contrast the styles of African American and white baseball. The African American player, as historian Robert Peterson notes, "had retained the gambling, rough, unorthodox style of play reminiscent of the days when [Ty] Cobb flew into second basemen with his spikes high and razor sharp.

Ty Cobb

African American pitchers threw more and different pitches, including those delivered with a ball greased, cut, coarsened, or in some way 'doctored.' They devised every motion conceivable: side-winder deliveries, submarine, cross-fire, even countless

One Man's Story of that Homer Hit at Yankee Stadium

Though we will probably never be certain whether Gibson hit a ball out of Yankee Stadium, Jack Marshall, of the Chicago American Giants, claims he saw him do it: "In 1934, Josh Gibson hit a ball off of Slim Jones in Yankee Stadium in a four-team doubleheader that we had there . . . They say a ball has never been hit out of Yankee Stadium. Well, that is a lie! Josh hit the ball over that triple deck next to the bullpen in left field. Over and out! I will never forget that because we were going down to Hightstown, New Jersey, to play a night game and we were standing in the aisle when that boy hit this ball!"

versions of hesitation pitches. Rules were arbitrary or not at all enforced, the only object was to win by getting the batter out."

African American players also played with a reckless but skilled style that the white players hadn't seen in years in their own leagues. Called "tricky baseball," the rules of strategy and logic were considered an inconvenience and weren't always followed. Bunts, intentional walks, and pick-off plays came at odd moments. This was all a stark contrast to the much more subdued game of the white players.

Despite the segregation of African American and white players at this time, and the routine

Philadelphia A's slugger Jimmie Foxx was one of many white baseball players who spoke openly about their high regard for Negro league baseball.

racism African American players experienced from many white players and white fans, a certain respect developed between African American and white ballplayers. White stars such as Dean and Foxx often praised certain African American players or the African American style of play to the press. And the great pitcher Walter Johnson had this to say about Gibson: "There is a catcher that any big-league club would like to buy for $200,000. His name is Gibson . . . he can do everything. He hits the ball a mile. And he catches so easy he might as well be in a rocking chair. Throws like a rifle. Bill Dickey isn't as good a catcher. Too bad this Gibson is a colored fellow."

Generally though, anti-African American sentiment among most major leaguers, especially among team owners, was overwhelming. The most notable example of a white player who hated African American players was Chicago White Stockings (later the White Sox) star Cap Anson. Anson played in the 1880s and 1890s, and was the first player to reach 3,000 career hits. Anson led a campaign against the presence of African American players in the major leagues at the time. In 1887, before his White Stockings were to play the New York Giants, who were led by African American pitching power George Stovey, Anson announced that his team would refuse to play against a team that fielded an African American player. The game didn't take place, and Anson's continued efforts over the years helped to insure the late bloom of African American participation in the major leagues.

Gibson, like many African American players, found some respite from this racism south of the border. Upon completing his first season with the Grays, in 1930 he began what would become another yearly ritual: He played winter ball in South America. When the season in South America ended, he returned to Pittsburgh to work odd jobs.

The next year, while still with the Grays, Gibson was credited with hitting seventy-five home runs, two more than the record-breaking Barry Bonds of the San Francisco Giants hit in

2001. As with all Negro league records, that mark is hard to verify, as league regulations differed and record keeping was limited in Gibson's day. By the end of his second year with the Grays, however, Gibson was a star and as such was selected to his first all-star game.

Babe Ruth watches the flight of one of his home runs. Josh
Gibson earned the nickname the "Black Babe Ruth" because of
his towering home runs and his commanding presence in the
Negro leagues.

The Black Babe Ruth, the White Josh Gibson

Members of the press often referred to Gibson as the "Black Babe Ruth," comparing Gibson's amazing home runs to those of white baseball's greatest longball hitter. Historians still use the description today, even though it implies that his skills are only valid when compared to those of a white athlete. Why not, Josh Jr. once asked, turn the equation around? As he said, "Why do they say Josh Gibson is the Black Babe Ruth? Why don't they say Babe Ruth is the white man's Josh Gibson?" In any case, it wasn't long before Gibson became a superstar.

Greenlee's Giants

An important development in Gibson's career occurred in 1931, when the then unknown businessman and gambler William A. "Gus" Greenlee purchased the Crawford Giants—the same sandlot team Gibson had helped to create and played for three years earlier. Greenlee had flash and a great sense of showmanship that he brought to the game of baseball. Later in 1931, Greenlee purchased the contract of Satchel Paige from the dissolved Cleveland Cubs for $250. This sum represented a significant increase in the salaries the current Giants were making, and was a sign of Greenlee's willingness to spend money in order to win.

Greenlee's next order of business further confirmed his bravado and commitment to African American baseball. At that time, African American baseball teams played their games in ballparks owned by white teams. The African American team would arrange, with a white owner, to play their games on the days white teams were out of town. These teams paid a rental charge and often a percentage of the gate receipts to the white owner. Greenlee, who was already establishing himself not only as a team owner but as an African American rights activist, took his team ownership to the next level: He built his team a stadium, Greenlee Field, with $100,000 out of his own pockets.

In 1932, Greenlee hoped to acquire the cream of Negro league baseball players. He raided the Homestead Grays, signing Oscar Charleston to be the Craws' player-manager. He snared Grays third baseman Judy Johnson, outfielder Ted Page, and added pitcher Sam Streeter. He then set his sights on Josh Gibson.

Greenlee and Cum Posey, the owner of the Grays, were two of the biggest names in African American baseball. Knowing that Greenlee would approach Gibson with an irresistible deal, Posey offered Gibson a contract the night before Greenlee did. Gibson signed the contract, thus (Posey thought) insuring Gibson's presence on the Grays' 1932 roster. But Gibson broke his contract with Posey after Greenlee approached him again. The lure of a little more money, a new ballpark, and the vitality that always accompanies the start of a new team proved too strong. Gibson boarded a bus and headed to Hot Springs, Arkansas, to begin spring training with the Crawfords.

The Craws were an independent team, meaning they did not have to play an organized schedule of games. Greenlee felt that more money could be made if the team's schedule remained flexible. The team traveled in a flashy new bus Greenlee had purchased, and employed a historian to keep records of all of their games and send news dispatches back to Pittsburgh area papers. The legend of the Crawfords spread rapidly, and the Craws played 94 games in 109 days between March 25 and July 21, 1932. They logged 17,000 miles on the road, and headed north to Pittsburgh for a dramatic match against the Grays.

Pittsburgh area fans, writers, and players eagerly anticipated the five-game series between the Craws and Grays. Greenlee and Posey undoubtedly saw the series as an opportunity for revenge. Despite losing players to Greenlee, Posey had put together a good team composed of wise veterans. In contrast, the Craws team was young and inexperienced, but exceptionally talented.

The series was evenly matched, and the Crawfords ended up winning three of five games. The 1932 series marked the beginning of a great rivalry that revved up local fans and infused African American baseball with a much-needed vitality. Posey couldn't deny that the advent of the Crawfords was beneficial for his team, especially since whenever the two teams played, he made the most money.

Off-Season

In 1933, Gibson spent the winter playing baseball in Latin America, joining white, African American, and Latino players from places like Mexico, Cuba, and Puerto Rico. It

was a winter season of blind baseball in which
players of all colors played on mixed teams.
Like most African American players playing
winter ball, Gibson joined these teams because
he loved the game and also because he needed
the money. Many white players also joined and
while playing on the same field against their
African American counterparts came to realize
that African American players were easily their
equals. Gibson preferred Puerto Rico out of all
the Latin American countries he played in
during the off-season. He fast became a hero to
local fans, and eventually a monument to
Gibson was placed in center field of San Juan's
Escambron Stadium, a place in which he had
hit many tape-measured home runs.

In 1933, Greenlee decided to form a new
league. He brought Posey's Grays team, along
with several other established teams, into what
he called the Negro National League. However,
African American and white team owners alike
were feeling the effects of the Depression. Babe
Ruth, the highest paid baseball player by far,

Josh Gibson *(right)* and Oscar Charleston pose in their Crawford Giants uniforms soon after joining the team in 1932.

took a $25,000 pay cut that year. Greenlee and other African American team owners realized that, despite the birth of their new league, the near future would be lean.

Times were tough, but they always had been, and for Gibson that just meant getting by and playing his beloved game. At the same time, Satchel Paige's fan and media appeal exploded. This brash, boisterous pitcher became the most famous African American player in the game. Sports writers loved him and his occasional crazy antics; he once left the Crawfords to take a bigger paycheck with a team in South Dakota, only to leave that team and rejoin the Craws. Although owner Greenlee was angry, he wouldn't dream of turning out his best pitcher and biggest draw.

Gibson was much more subdued, and was often called a "player's player" by his teammates, with whom he was very close. Though the press loved to write about Gibson's miraculous homers, he didn't draw crowds of fans like Paige. This would soon affect Gibson's professional fortunes.

With Paige and Gibson on the same team, something had to give. Gibson was a favorite of the other Craws, while Paige mostly kept to himself—a sign of his maverick personality. It became clear, at least to Greenlee, that one of them would have to be traded for financial reasons. Gibson was one of the top stars of African American baseball, perhaps the biggest next to Paige. Though he was the opposite in every way to the colorful Paige, Gibson was one of the league's greatest hitters and received nearly as much press coverage as Paige. In other words, Gibson knew his worth, or so he thought. One mistake Gibson made was in judging his worth as a player but not as an entertainer.

Nevertheless, Gibson's contribution to the Crawfords was immense. Because of the general lack of official records for nearly the entire history of Negro league seasons, relating Gibson's accomplishments on the field with certainty is difficult. Luckily, Greenlee had employed someone to keep track of the

Crawfords' seasons. In 1933, Gibson played in 137 games for the Crawfords. He came to the plate 512 times. He had 239 hits, which gave him a batting average of .467, nearly 100 points higher than his next closest teammate. Gibson also led the team in triples and home runs (with 55), and was second on the team in runs scored.

These impressive numbers reflect the importance of Gibson to a team that was already one of the best in Negro baseball—an importance not lost on Gibson. The average salary for an African American player during the Depression was a meager $125 a month, but Gibson was well paid, making $250 to $400 a month.

To some, however, the money African American players made in comparison to their white counterparts was a product of something other than the economic hardship that had swept the country. Johnny Drew, the African American owner of the Philadelphia Hilldale team, put the blame on African American owners and players for underestimating their own worth. As he put it, "For [the African American ballplayer], there has never been any future, nobody has ever thought of making it possible for him to earn a salary of five

Gus Greenlee

thousand dollars a year. He has been exploited and bamboozled by the very men for whom he made fortunes in the past."

Drew also pointed to African American fans as part of the problem, calling them hypocrites for complaining of the increased price of admission to African American games—a move the owners had to make to attempt to break even. But these fans paid just as much money to attend games in which African American teams played white all-star teams. In other words, the economics of African American baseball were complicated.

Important Statistics from Josh Gibson's Career

- Seasons played: 1930–1946, Homestead Grays, Crawford Giants
- Lifetime batting average: .347
- Career home runs: 962
- Number of all-star appearances: 9
- Number of pennants: at least 7
- Career batting average in all-star games: .483
- Home run championships: 9
- Batting titles: 4

Regardless of the source of the economic problems African American baseball faced, the Crawfords were dangerously close to folding. The team had never turned a profit, despite their famous lineup and flashy showmanship. By 1937, things worsened for the team, as a bidding war for Gibson's services began. While Gibson was in Puerto Rico playing winter ball, two teams, the

Philadelphia Stars and the Homestead Grays, had offered Gibson different packages. The Stars offered Gibson a higher salary to be player-manager of their club. The Grays offered $2,500 and two players to the Craws in exchange for Gibson and Judy Johnson.

Hardball

When Gibson returned home, he held out for the best offer, a fairly uncommon practice at the time and certainly out of character for him. Gibson realized that he had to take a stand. He wanted to obtain a contract that would pay him what he thought he was worth. He was tired of the long seasons, and he was being paid far less than what he was worth as the top hitter in the game. The hardball between Gibson and the Craws began.

In an attempt to lessen Gibson's value in the eyes of the public, and perhaps in Gibson's eyes as well, John L. Clark, Greenlee's secretary and spokesperson, wrote the following

Josh Gibson *(standing, second from right)* rejoined the Homestead Grays in 1937 after one of the most notable trades in Negro league history.

in a column published in Pittsburgh's African American newspaper, the *Courier:* "He is an asset to any club. But not the kind of asset more colorful and less capable players might be. With all of his ability, he has not developed that which pulls the cash

customers through the turnstiles . . . although he has been publicized as much as Satchel Paige." Most people ignored these comments and felt that Gibson had proven his value. Finally, the Grays' offer came through, and Gibson became, in what the *Courier* called "the biggest player deal in the history of Negro baseball," a Homestead Gray once again.

Josh Gibson's humble resting place in Allegheny Cemetery in Pittsburgh, Pennsylvania

The Early Death of a Star

*He was a big, overgrown kid who was glad
for the chance he had. He loved his life.*

—Ted Page, Gibson's former Grays teammate

Before discussing the circumstances surrounding Gibson's death, it is important to look at an event that occurred a few years before. It was a time when Gibson had begun a downward spiral, and could be called the most critical moment in African American baseball history. The setting was the recently revived Negro League World Series in 1933. The competing teams were the Kansas City Monarchs, led by

Satchel Paige, and the Homestead Grays with Josh Gibson as their undeclared, quiet leader.

The Monarchs, thanks to Paige's superb pitching, easily won Game 1, 8–0. In Game 2, Paige came on to pitch, relieving Hilton Smith. The Monarchs led 2–0. In the seventh inning, Paige gave up a single to Jerry Benjamin, and it was then that Paige's interior wheels began to spin. Always the showman, Paige called his first baseman, Buck O'Neill, over to the pitching mound and explained that he wanted to walk the next two batters, Howard Easterling and Buck Leonard. Paige wanted to face Josh Gibson with the bases loaded, creating in this one at-bat a defining moment in the history of African American baseball.

O'Neill couldn't believe what he was hearing, but the Monarchs' manager, Frank Duncan, who had also come to the mound, agreed with Paige. As he said, "Listen, Buck. You know all these people we got in this ballpark? They came out to see Satchel Paige and Josh Gibson. So whatever he wanna do, let him do it." Additionally, Paige knew something that most players, especially pitchers, had come to realize about Gibson. Unknown to most fans, Gibson was not the same hitter he had been several years before, when he seemingly had no fear at the plate.

The Downward Spiral

Since Gibson had been playing winter ball in Latin America for most of his professional career, his trip to Mexico the previous winter was not unusual. Unfortunately, while he was there, his abuse of alcohol increased. While playing in Veracruz, he would sit in the dugout and drink one beer after another between games with his teammate, Sam Bankhead. Gibson also developed a new, much more serious appetite: He began to experiment with heroin.

Most evidence attributes this abrupt turn in Gibson's life to his failed relationship with a woman named Hattie, who lived with Gibson and had become his common-law wife. She had been effective, while they were together, in keeping Gibson together. When they separated, Gibson began an affair with a married woman from Washington, D.C., named Grace Fournier. Fournier was a heavy drinker and known narcotics user. The couple had too many bad habits in common.

Gibson often complained in those days of being tired and ill, and many people involved with the Grays commented that he looked nervous and bewildered most of the time. He had definitely changed, even his body. He went from being the lean, muscled athlete who used to inspire awe from all who saw him, to a fat 225 pounds, with most of his weight seemingly contained in his belly. Cum Posey, who still owned the Grays, would let Gibson play even if he had been drinking, if only because he could still hit with the best of them. That year, Gibson had hit .323 in league games and led the league with 11 home runs in 41 games; the next year he led the league, reportedly hitting .521, with 14 homers.

Gibson's Grays teammate, Buck Leonard, also enjoyed a stellar career in the Negro leagues and was eventually inducted into Major League Baseball's Hall of Fame.

But pitchers had learned of Gibson's self-destructive behaviors, and many players figured out that they could get into Gibson's head, make him think too much while at the plate, and strike him out. At least this is what Paige was thinking when he arranged to face Gibson with the bases loaded in the Negro League World Series.

Showdown

Legend has it that once Gibson got into the hitter's box, Paige began to distract him with "trash talk." He would tell Gibson what kind of pitch he was going to make, and where it would be placed. Gibson, unsure of Paige's words and also just plain bewildered, watched three fastballs sail past him. He was out. According to the papers, Gibson had swung at two pitches, fouling off the first two, before swinging again and missing the third. Either way, one newspaper's headline the next day told the whole story: "Satch Fans Josh Gibson With Three on Bases."

This story is emblematic of the problems that Gibson faced throughout his life, particularly his baseball life. He was never quite able to get out from under Paige's shadow. Nor was he able to summon a suitable destiny for himself. Gibson's life was a series of painful episodes marked by an occasional high point on the ball field. His alcohol and drug problems and his physical deterioration made him vulnerable in such a competitive sport.

Blackout

New Year's Day, 1943. Gibson had been complaining of splitting headaches for a few weeks. He assumed the headaches resulted from his constant drinking binges. But on that day, he fell into a coma that lasted for six hours. His doctors at Pittsburgh's St. Francis Hospital publicly declared his problem to be exhaustion. Gibson left ten days later, and not much more was made of it.

Gibson took the advice of his doctors and manager and rested. He seemed to rebound that year, hitting .526 that season, and had a three-home-run game, including one that reportedly sailed 460 feet. Things seemed, if not great, then at least OK, except for his considerable drinking problem. He was still hitting balls all over the field, still playing in most of the Grays' games. To an outsider, Gibson probably seemed like the player he had always been.

But he was not. Though most of the people associated with African American baseball knew Gibson was having substance abuse problems—and most of them were upset that the player who represented all that was good in the league was in sharp decline—little about it was spoken outright. The next year, Gibson's power decreased dramatically. For the first time in his playing career, he became a "singles hitter." He was knocking fewer home runs, and many assumed that his power loss was due to drinking and aging.

Since Cum Posey tightly controlled press coverage about Gibson, the fans knew next to nothing about Gibson's decline. The papers reported that he was taking a "rest," when he was actually spending time in various sanatoriums closely monitored by doctors and nurses. Posey feared that Gibson was losing his mind. These sanatorium visits soon became a regular part of Gibson's life.

As it turned out, exhaustion had not caused Gibson's New Year's Day blackout. Doctors informed him that he had a brain tumor. Gibson never let on about this fact, and continued to play when he could. Unfortunately, he also continued to shoot heroin and drink, often getting into trouble with police, who frequently took him away in a straitjacket.

Gibson continued to miss more games, including the 1945 East-West All-Star Game. Apparently, he hadn't been able to find his way to Chicago, where the game was played. Gibson also became suicidal. He began talking to imaginary people, and continued drinking.

He played his last games in the fall and winter of 1946 in the Puerto Rican League, but Gibson's most notable times that season took place off the field in local bars, where he would drink himself into a rage and often end up in the local jail. These bouts with booze led to his arrest one evening after he was found walking naked through the streets in a daze. The police asked him what he was doing and Gibson replied that he was trying to get to the airport. He was placed in a local sanatorium, released, and sent back to Pittsburgh.

While Gibson spent the winter in Puerto Rico—and frequently in trouble—the American baseball world swelled with the anticipation that Jackie Robinson was going to join the Brooklyn Dodgers. Robinson was the first African American baseball player since Moses "Fleet" Walker to play in the major leagues. For a time, many felt that Gibson might be the first Negro league player to join the majors.

Gibson had wanted to play in the big leagues because it would have given him the chance to

Jackie Robinson and Branch Rickey, owner of the Brooklyn Dodgers, shake hands after signing a contract for Robinson's second season with the team—and a $10,000 increase in salary—in 1948.

show the world that African American baseball players were the equals of, if not superior to, white players. Given a chance to cross the color line, it seems fair to say Gibson would have had an impact on the major leagues. But by the time white owners were beginning to seriously consider integrating their league, Gibson and other Negro league stars, like Satchel Paige and

Cool Papa Bell, were nearing the end of their playing careers.

A Great Loss

The end was near, and Gibson tried to reconnect with his family. He had barely seen his children during their childhood. Due in large part to Gibson's failure to offer any kind of financial support to his former mother-in-law, who was raising the children, they had grown up in poverty.

By 1947, Gibson was gravely ill, suffering from high blood pressure and bronchitis in addition to his other ailments. He had moved into his mother's house, back home in Pittsburgh's North Side. A few weeks later, on Sunday, January 19, Gibson went to see a movie at the Garden Theater and fell unconscious in his seat. He died in his bed at 1:30 AM the next day, with his sister, Annie Mahaffery, and his younger brother, Jerry, at his side. The cause of death, as filed by the doctor on the scene, was a stroke. Gibson died young, poor, and in many ways, alone. Though his family was with him, he barely knew them.

His funeral attracted numerous ball players, word of his death having spread quickly across the country. Though some players were still in Latin America playing winter ball, many of Gibson's teammates attended his funeral. Many reporters claimed that Gibson had died of a broken heart, and that he was bitter and broken because he had never been able to play alongside his white peers. If Gibson died of a broken heart, it is likely that his sadness was due more to his distant relationship with his family, especially his children. In either case, the world of baseball, African American and white, had lost one of its greatest players.

Satchel Paige stands by the plaque commemorating his induction into Major League Baseball's Hall of Fame on August 9, 1971.

Negro League Baseball Arrives

On August 9, 1971, Satchel Paige became the first Negro league player elected into Major League Baseball's Hall of Fame. Six years earlier, the splendid white player Ted Williams was inducted to the Hall of Fame. During his induction speech, Williams remarked, "Baseball gives every American boy a chance to excel. This is the nature of man and the name of the game. I hope that someday Satchel Paige and Josh Gibson will be voted into the Hall of Fame as symbols of the great Negro players who are not here only because they weren't given the chance."

Jackie Robinson had crossed the color line years before and had been inducted into the

Hall of Fame in 1962. Many Latino and African American players had long and impressive major league careers after him, among them Hall-of-Famers Frank Robinson, Willie Mays, Hank Aaron, and Roberto Clemente. But finally, in 1969, the Baseball Writers Association, the group that voted members into the Hall, created a special Negro leagues panel in order to redress these grievances. Satchel Paige, African American baseball's most famous son, was the logical first choice.

Since Paige's election, sixteen more Negro league players have been elected into the Hall of Fame, including Josh Gibson, who was elected the following year. The Baseball Hall of Fame Committee on Baseball Veterans, a panel comprised of writers and Hall of Fame players that votes on players overlooked in the regular polling, took over the duties of the Negro leagues panel. In a special amendment to the Veterans Committee rules, two special elections were held each year from 1995 through 1999, one of which was exclusively for Negro league players. That term was extended two years, and still existed as of the 2001 elections, when Smokey Joe Williams was elected.

The Gibson family—Josh Jr. and his family, and Josh Sr.'s sister, Annie—accepted the posthumous tribute to Gibson in 1972 at the Hall of Fame in Cooperstown, New York. They called Gibson's induction "a beautiful thing," and made their way back to Pittsburgh, where life was still tough and they still lived in poverty.

The Negro Leagues Baseball Museum

The Negro Leagues Baseball Museum (NLBM) opened in Kansas City, Missouri, in January 1991. Located in the historic Vine District adjacent to the Jazz Museum, the NLBM has become an important voice in the preservation of African American baseball history. Though not an official hall of fame, the museum features a 10,000 square-foot multimedia exhibit. It includes two film exhibits, two video exhibits, and fifteen interactive computer stations.

The museum gallery is arranged as a timeline of African American and baseball history, from the 1860s to the 1950s. The centerpiece is the "Field of Legends," which features twelve life-sized bronze cast sculptures of the most important players in Negro leagues history. The statues stand at each position on the field, and the one behind the plate depicts African American baseball's greatest catcher, Josh Gibson.

Baseball Today

Today, baseball seems to have overcome many of racism's effects. White players are now in the minority in professional baseball. In addition to the talented African American and Latino players, many Asian players, such as Hideo Nomo and Ichiro Suzuki from countries like Korea and Japan, where baseball is a huge national favorite pastime, have made their way

Negro League Players Elected to the Baseball Hall of Fame

Satchel Paige, pitcher, 1971, Negro Leagues Panel

Josh Gibson, catcher, 1972, Negro Leagues Panel

Buck Leonard, first base, 1972, Negro Leagues Panel

Monte Irvin, left field, 1973, Negro Leagues Panel

Cool Papa Bell, center field, 1974, Negro Leagues Panel

Judy Johnson, third base, 1975, Negro Leagues Panel

Oscar Charleston, first base-center field, 1976,
    Negro Leagues Panel

Martin Dihigo, pitcher-outfield, 1977, Negro Leagues Panel

Pop Lloyd, shortstop, 1977, Negro Leagues Panel

Rube Foster, pitcher-manager, 1981, Veterans Committee

Ray Dandridge, third base, 1987, Veterans Committee

Leon Day, pitcher-second base-outfield, 1995,
    Veterans Committee

Willie Wells, shortstop, 1997, Veterans Committee

Wilber Rogan, pitcher, 1998, Veterans Committee

Joe Williams, pitcher, 1999, Veterans Committee

Turkey Stearnes, center field, 2000, Veterans Committee

Hilton Smith, pitcher, 2001, Veterans Committee

onto major league rosters. Jim Crow laws grudgingly disappeared off state law books; civil rights became a national issue. The playing field, perhaps, has been leveled. But this is not to say that racism does not exist in this country in more subtle ways.

But in baseball, at least, minority players have a home. Current African American and Latino players such as Ken Griffey Jr., Sammy Sosa, Alex Rodriguez, and Barry Bonds could not have played in the major leagues sixty years ago. Today, they are among the game's top stars, highest wage earners, and biggest fan favorites.

There is still the occasional racist outburst, such as when Atlanta Braves relief pitcher John Rocker lashed out against minorities to a reporter during the months before the 2000 season. Rocker's remarks caused a stir in the press and among baseball players, fans, and executives. But overall, public outbursts happen far less frequently than when Jackie Robinson played his first season with the Brooklyn Dodgers.

So when you're watching your favorite team, whether on television or at the ballpark, think about Josh Gibson, the Negro leagues, and how far today's minority players have come in the struggle for integration. The importance of Gibson's determination, integrity, and awesome skill cannot be underestimated. The legacy of Josh Gibson remains with us in many ways: in the historical marker the city of Pittsburgh created in his honor, for instance, and in the Josh Gibson Little League.

Perhaps most important, the memory of Josh Gibson is preserved in Pittsburgh with each swing every minority player takes, whether in the big leagues or to knock a pitch across a dusty sandlot as the sun sets and dinnertime approaches. Josh Gibson and the Negro leagues will forever hold a place in the history of baseball.

Timeline

1846 The first recorded baseball game takes place between the Knickerbocker Base Ball Club of New York and the New York Base Ball Club, at Elysian Fields in Hoboken, New Jersey.

1860 Two African American baseball teams, Weeksville of New York and the Colored Union Club, play in Brooklyn.

1866 The Southern League of Colored Base Ballists becomes the first Negro league.

1878 Pitcher John "Bud" Fowler becomes the first African American player to cross the minor league color barrier.

1883 Moses "Fleet" Fleetwood Walker and his brother Welday sign with the Toledo Blue Stockings of the Northwestern League.

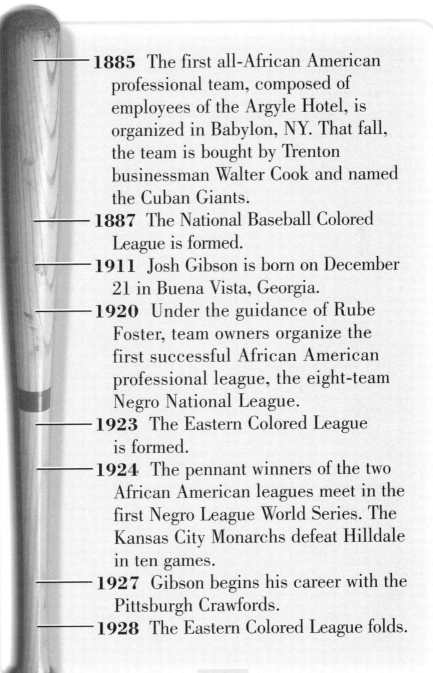

1885 The first all-African American professional team, composed of employees of the Argyle Hotel, is organized in Babylon, NY. That fall, the team is bought by Trenton businessman Walter Cook and named the Cuban Giants.

1887 The National Baseball Colored League is formed.

1911 Josh Gibson is born on December 21 in Buena Vista, Georgia.

1920 Under the guidance of Rube Foster, team owners organize the first successful African American professional league, the eight-team Negro National League.

1923 The Eastern Colored League is formed.

1924 The pennant winners of the two African American leagues meet in the first Negro League World Series. The Kansas City Monarchs defeat Hilldale in ten games.

1927 Gibson begins his career with the Pittsburgh Crawfords.

1928 The Eastern Colored League folds.

1930 Gibson begins to play for the Homestead Grays.

1932 The Negro National League shuts down after twelve seasons.

1933 Gus Greenlee organizes the second Negro National League. The first Negro League all-star game takes place in Chicago.

1937 The Negro American League is formed with teams in Chicago, Kansas City, Detroit, Indianapolis, Cincinnati, St. Louis, Memphis, and Birmingham. The Kansas City Monarchs win five of the first six NAL pennants. In the NNL, the Homestead Grays win eight pennants between 1937–1945.

1937 Gibson plays in the Dominican Republic for dictator Rafael Trujillo.

1938 Gibson wins his first batting title with a batting average of .440.

1942 The Negro League World Series is played for the first time since 1927. The Monarchs sweep the Grays in four games.

1943 Gibson blacks out and is hospitalized on New Year's Day.

1945 Jackie Robinson signs a contract to play for the Brooklyn Dodgers' minor league team, the Montreal Royals.

1947 On January 20, Josh Gibson dies of a brain tumor only a month after his thirty-fifth birthday.

1947 Jackie Robinson plays in the major leagues and wins the National League Rookie of the Year Award.

1949 The Negro American League absorbs the Negro National League, which folded in 1948 due to poor attendance and fewer quality players to choose from, as more and more African American players were jumping to the major leagues.

1963 The Negro American League folds. Organized African American baseball is relegated to a few traveling teams.

1972 Gibson is inducted into the Baseball Hall of Fame.

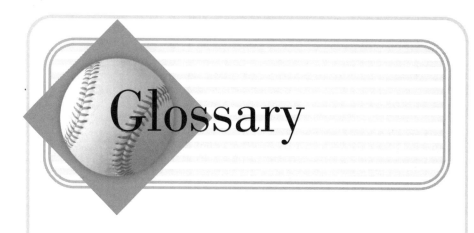

Glossary

apprentice An inexperienced person who learns by practical experience under the instruction of a more experienced person.

batting average A measure of a batter's performance taken by dividing the total number of hits by the number of times at bat, not including walks.

destiny A predetermined course of events beyond an individual's power to change.

dislocation A displacement of bones from their normal position near a joint.

gentleman's agreement In baseball, a silent agreement between many white team owners not to allow African American players onto their teams.

Great Depression Economic slump in North America, Europe, and other industrialized areas of the world that began in 1929 and lasted until about 1939. It was the longest and most severe depression ever experienced by the industrialized Western world.

induction The process of bringing someone into a group.

Jim Crow Any of the laws that enforced racial segregation in the U.S. South between the end of the formal Reconstruction period in 1877 and the beginning of a strong civil rights movement in the 1950s.

mausoleum A long tomb or a stone structure enclosing a place of burial.

narcotic A drug that in moderate doses dulls the senses, relieves pain, and induces profound sleep, but in excessive doses can cause stupor, coma, or convulsions.

Plessy v. Ferguson An 1896 court case in which the Supreme Court handed down the decision that "legislation is powerless to eradicate racial instincts." This made into law the doctrine supporting "separate but equal" accommodations.

Reconstruction In U.S. history, the period during and after the American Civil War (1865–1877) in which attempts were made to solve the political, social, and economic problems arising from the readmission to the Union of the eleven Confederate states that had seceded at or before the outbreak of war.

repeal To revoke or rescind, that is, render invalid.

sanatorium An institution for rest and recuperation, often for the treatment of people with chronic illnesses.

segregation Separation of groups of people from one another.

straitjacket A heavy jacket with straps to restrict the movement of arms, used to restrain violent or mentally ill people.

For More Information

National Baseball Hall of Fame
25 Main Street
P.O. Box 590
Cooperstown, NY 13326
(888) HALL-OF-FAME (425-5633)
Web site: http://baseballhalloffame.org

National Civil Rights Museum
Lorraine Motel
450 Mulberry Street
Memphis, TN 38103-4214
(901) 521-9699
Web site: http://216.157.9.6/civilrights

Negro League Baseball Museum
1616 E. 18th Street
Kansas City, MO 64108-1610
(816) 221-1920
Web site: http://www.nlbm.com

Web Sites

The African-American Mosaic: A Library of
    Congress Resource Guide for the Study of
    Black History and Culture
http://lcweb.loc.gov/exhibits/african/intro.html

Black Baseball's Negro Baseball Leagues
http://www.blackbaseball.com

Library of Congress: American Memories, By
    Popular Demand: Jackie Robinson and Other
    Baseball Highlights, 1860s–1960s
http://lcweb2.loc.gov/ammem/jrhtml

Negro League Baseball.com: Negro League
    Baseball Frequently Asked Questions
http://www.negroleaguebaseball.com/faq.html

Negro Leagues Baseball Museum, via the Kansas
   City Star
http://www.kcstar.com/sports/museum

Shadowball
http://www.negroleague.columbus.oh.us/extras.htm

Videos
Burns, Ken. *Baseball: Shadowball,* Episode 5.
   New York: PBS Home Video, 1994.

Davidson, Craig. *There Was Always Sun Shining
   Someplace: Life in the Negro Baseball Leagues.*
   Narrated by James Earl Jones. Westport, CT:
   Refocus Films, 1984.

Sullivan, Kevin Rodney. *Soul of the Game.* New
   York: HBO Studios, 1996.

Winfield, Paul. *Only the Ball Was White.* Orlando
   Park, IL: MPI Home Video, 1994.

For Further Reading

Brashler, William. *Josh Gibson: A Life in the Negro Leagues.* Chicago: Ivan R. Dee, 2000.

Dixon, Phil S., and Patrick J. Hannigan. *The Negro Baseball Leagues: A Photographic History.* Mattituck, NY: Amereon House, 1992.

McKissack, Patricia C., and Fredrick McKissack. *Black Diamond: The Story of the Negro Baseball Leagues.* New York: Scholastic, 1998.

O'Neil, Buck, et al. *I Was Right on Time.* New York: Simon & Schuster, 1996.

Peterson, Robert. *Only the Ball Was White.* New York: Oxford University Press, 1970.

Riley, James A. *The Biographical Encyclopedia of the Negro Baseball Leagues.* New York: Carroll & Graf, 1994.

For Advanced Readers

Ribowsky, Mark. *A Complete History of the Negro Leagues: 1884 to 1955.* New York: Birch Lane Press, 1995.

Ribowsky, Mark. *The Power and the Darkness: The Life of Josh Gibson in the Shadows of the Game.* New York: Simon & Schuster, 1996.

Index

A

American Negro League, 33
Anson, Cap, 57–58

B

Baseball Hall of Fame, Major
    League, 91–93
baseball history, early, 11–22
Bell, James "Cool Papa," 23, 88
Bonds, Barry, 58, 96

C

Catto, Octavius V., 13, 14, 15
Charleston, Oscar, 63
Cleveland, Grover, 22
Colored Union Club, 11
Crawford Colored Giants (Craws),
    36–37, 38, 62, 64–65, 68,
    69–70, 72
Cuban Giants, 19–20

D

Dean, Dizzy, 54, 57
Dickey, Bill, 57
Drew, Johnny, 70–71

E

Ewing, Buck, 38, 48, 49

F

Foster, Rube, 31, 32–33
Fowler, John "Bud," 17, 18,
    19, 21
Foxx, Jimmie, 54, 57

G

Gehrig, Lou, 41
Gibson, Josh
    death and burial, 5, 7–8, 9, 76,
        77–89
    family, 27, 35, 52–53,
        88–89, 93
    statistics from baseball games of,
        6, 51, 55, 69–70, 72, 80, 84
Gibson, Josh Jr. (son), 53, 61, 93
Gibson, Mark (father), 26–27
Greenlee, William A. "Gus,"
    62–65, 67, 69–70

H

Harris, Vic, 38, 47, 48

Homestead Grays, 28–29, 31, 32, 36, 38, 46–59, 63–65, 66, 73, 74, 75

I

International League, 21

J

Johnson, Judy, 38, 47–48, 63, 73
Johnson, Walter, 57

K

Knickerbocker Base Ball Club, 11

L

Lang, John F., 20
Leonard, Buck, 78

M

Mantle, Mickey, 51
Marshall, Jack, 55
Mason, Helen (wife), 51–53

N

National Association of Base Ball Players (NABBL), 13–14
National Association of Professional Base Ball Players (NAPBBL), 16–17
Negro Leagues Baseball Museum, 93–94
Negro National League, 31–33, 47, 66
New York Base Ball Club, 11
New York Times, 22

P

Page, Ted, 63, 77
Paige, Satchel, 7, 23, 45–46, 62, 67, 69, 75, 78–79, 82, 87, 91, 92
Philadelphia Athletics, 14
Philadelphia Independent, 50
Phillips, Horace, 21
Pittsburgh Courier, 37, 38, 74, 75
Plessy v. Ferguson, 22
Posey, Cumberland "Cum" Willis, 28–31, 32, 47, 48, 49, 63–65, 66, 80, 85
Pythians, 13, 14, 15

R

racism, 8, 14–15, 17–18, 21–22, 23, 25–26, 56–58, 70–71
Robinson, Jackie, 86, 91–92, 96
Ruth, Babe (George Herman), 5–6, 51, 61, 66–68

S

Simmons, Harry, 10, 11
Southern League, 19
Sporting Life, 18
Stovey, George, 19, 58
Streeter, Sam, 63

W

Walker, Moses Fleetwood "Fleet," 17, 18, 19, 21, 86
Weeksville, 11
Williams, Smokey Joe, 29, 47, 93
Williams, Ted, 91
Wilson, W. Rollo, 50

About the Author

Nicholas Twemlow is a freelance writer and filmmaker living in Brooklyn, New York. After completing a Master of Fine Arts in creative writing at the University of Iowa Writers' Workshop, he worked for an online sports magazine as a writer and editor, interviewing figures from across the world of sports, including the infamous Pete Rose. He also served as a correspondent at the 2000 running of NASCAR's Daytona 500. Tremlow has produced and edited several Web documentaries, among them a profile of boxer "Sugar" Shane Mosley and the weeks leading to the fighter's upset victory over Oscar De La Hoya. Twemlow grew up in Kansas, and calls the Kansas City Royals his favorite baseball team.

Photo Credits

Layout

Nelson Sá

Design

Claudia Carlson